A-B-C of Community Care

What it's really all about

by

Harry Tunnicliffe, George Coyle
&
Willie More

ISBN 0 948680 31 8

The Authors

This trio of authors have worked together over the years in a number a various guises in both training and publishing.

Harry Tunnicliffe, author of a number of books on the law relating to social work, was formerly a Principal Lecturer in Social Work at Birmingham Polytechnic. He has a background in child care, adoption and general social work but now works as an independent trainer and consultant.

George Coyle has a background in child care and general social work but for the past decade he has operated as a social work and training consultant and a guardian-ad-litem. Most recently he has been involved in training for community care. With Harry Tunnicliffe, George is Co-Editor of the journal, 'Law & Practice'

Willie More also has a background in residential care with both children and older people in a hospital setting. As well as offering a number of training programmes, he also manages PEPAR Publications, a small but significant publishing house for social work, social care and allied professions.

Acknowledgements

The authors wish to thank Robert Hogg, Director, and Alan Bates, Principal Training Officer, both of Walsall Social Services Department for their commission to produce the Community Care Training Pack which in turn spawned this publication. If it were not for them, this booklet would not exist.

January 1993

Contents Guide

Preface

In November 1992, Walsall Social Services Department commissioned PEPAR Publications to produce their training pack, "Community Care Training Programme". The task of writing and preparing was delegated to Harry Tunnicliffe, George Coyle and Willie More. The pack was so well received that PEPAR Publications was encouraged to reorganise the material as a primer-type booklet for a wider and national audience of social services departments, health authorities and trusts, housing departments, etc. This publication is the result. Any agency that wishes further information about the training pack should write to the publishers at the address on the back cover.

PEPAR Publications   **December 1992**

Chapter One

Background to the Act

In December 1986, Sir Roy Griffiths was requested by Norman Fowler (the then Secretary of State) to undertake the following task:

"To review the way in which public funds are used to support community care policy and to advise me (Secretary of State) on the options for action that would improve the use of these funds as a contribution to more effective community care."

The emphasis was that the review should be brief and geared towards advice on action (as was the previous review on Management of the Health Service 1983, "Working for Patients").

The review was clearly to be about more efficient and cost-effective community care. It was neither to deal with the level of funding nor about cost reduction, but it was to focus on how resources (at whatever level) could be better used to provide community care in a more effective manner.

The Griffiths Report is not a Royal Commission Report. It is based on a number of sources; in addition to his own team, Griffiths took numerous submissions from various other groups.

Some of these sources from which he drew are:

1. 1983: Review – Management of the Health Service, "Working for Patients" (many of its recommendations are to be found embedded in Sections 1 – 41 of the National Health Service and Community Care Act 1990)

2. 1985 (commissioned): Review – The Role of Residential Care (Lady Wagner) became "Residential Care: A Positive Choice" (published 1988)

3. 1984/85: House of Commons Social Services Committee Report (this was more specifically related to mentally ill and mentally handicapped people).

4. 1986: The Audit Commission Report, "Making a Reality of Community Care". This is of particular importance since a main conclusion was that better value could be obtained from existing resources; it also said that something had to be done – the status quo was not an option.

It was from the Social Services Committee Report and the Audit Commission Report that Griffiths basically drew his material, although he used other external submissions. It is also worth noting the influence of the Barclay Report (1983) in terms of the Purchaser/Provider concept.

The Griffiths Report (1988) eventually led to the White Paper in 1989 – 'Caring for People: Community Care in the Next Decade and Beyond'. This is the key document in relation to community care and it enshrines most of the Griffiths recommendations. The National Health Service and Community Care Act 1990 is simply the legal means of implementing the White Paper.

Sections 1 – 41 of the Act deal with NHS management and such issues as NHS Trusts and GP Fund-Holding Practices etc., and are therefore only indirectly related to community care for social services and health authority staff who will be part of the assessment, purchasing and delivery systems.

The Griffiths Report

Griffiths started his review by suggesting what might be wrong with existing community care – if in fact it really did exist!

> *"Community care has been talked of for thirty years and in few areas can the gap between political rhetoric and policy on the one hand, or between policy and reality in the field on the other hand, have been so great." (Griffiths)*

1. Responsibility is divided between Social Security (finance), Health (personal social services – through SSDs: medical – through HAs) and Department of Environment (housing mainly), leading to..."a feeling that community care is a poor relation; everybody's distant relative but nobody's baby."

2. The differences between medical and non-medical care. A person in need of medical care has one identified source of help – the GP, who may of course refer on. Medical care tends to offer what you need; it is more usually needs-led rather than resource-led. On the other hand, it is rare for one individual to take responsibility for non-medical needs and care, and non-medical services tend to be related to what is available, i.e. resource-led.

3. Although there have been some successes in the past, the history of joint planning and financing between local authorities and health authorities is far from reassuring.

4. The present system of residential care, whereby the client (i.e. older person, adult disabled, mother and baby, etc.) finds their own establishment (often without any assessment of need) and then, if eligible, claims all or part of the cost direct from social security (subject to upper limits) provides a 'perverse' incentive in favour of residential care. Financially the amounts paid by social security are much higher than those which could be claimed by the same person if they remained in the community.

5. Residential care is often a lottery – geriatric ward/nursing home/residential home – LA/voluntary/private? There is often no clear system as to allocation. It is often a matter of chance rather than planning according to needs – a common approach is required.

6. Community Care needs on discharge from or closure of hospitals, etc. are often not satisfactorily met. Often patients/clients are discharged without a clear package of care in place to meet their needs in the community, and frequently no one person is responsible for ensuring care.

> What do you think about Griffiths' concerns? Are they valid problems? – do they exist? – what other problems can you identify?

The Solution

Having identified the problems, Griffiths was then faced with identifying a solution.

He states that he could have suggested a radical solution such as totally changing the systems, i.e. health authorities to provide community care for discharged patients, or changing organisational structures between health authorities, social services departments etc. and many others He did not suggest any of these but decided to take a different approach which he sees as being even more radical.

Recommendations

1. In relation to the public sector, Central Government should:

   a) spell out clearly their responsibilities;

   b) insist on performance and make them accountable;

   c) require evidence on their action;

   d) match policy with resources;

   e) set timescales

   NB: Although Central Government already controls the public sector in many ways, particularly in terms of finance, it does not usually control them in the ways highlighted above. Usually the public sector authorities have autonomy to provide as they themselves decide within the financial and legal boundaries set by Central Government. It is because of this that Griffiths considers the approach to be radical.

2. The role of the social services department should change. Of particular importance is the key statement which emphasises its role of 'purchaser' as distinct to its traditional role of 'provider'. (This was one of the recommendations of the Barclay Report in 1983.)

At the local level the role of social service authorities should be re-orientated towards ensuring that :

• the needs of individuals within the specified groups are identified;

• packages of care are devised;

• services are co-ordinated;

• a specific care manager is assigned, where appropriate.

The type of services to be provided would be derived from analysis of the individual care needs.

The responsibility of social services authorities is to ensure that these services are provided within the appropriate budgets by public or private sector according to where they can be provided most economically and efficiently.

The onus in all cases should be on social services authorities to show that the private sector is being fully stimulated and encouraged and that competitive tenders or other means of testing the market are taken.

This is a key statement. The role of the public sector is essentially to ensure that care is provided. How it is provided is an important, but secondary, consideration and local authorities must show they are getting and providing real value.

As to residential accommodation, social services authorities should be responsible for assessing whether a move to such accommodation is in the best interests of the individual and what the local authority is prepared to pay for.

3. Community care is about the health as well as the social needs of the population. Health care, in its broadest sense, is an essential component of the range of services which may be needed to help people to continue to live in their own homes for as long as possible. The key functions and

responsibilities of the health service should remain essentially unaltered. 'Working for Patients' explained that it would be the responsibility of health authorities to ensure that the health needs of the population for which they are responsible are met, and this should include those people who also have a need for social care. They may well have special needs for health care, whether for primary care or acute hospital care, or for long-term care. Their handicap or disability may also make them heavy consumers of health care. In some individual cases it may well be difficult to draw a clear distinction between the needs of an individual for health and for social care. In such cases, it will be critically important for the responsible authorities to work together.

Many people have already expressed the opinion that community care can only be improved by a vast increase in resources, particularly in financial terms. Whilst in one sense this may be true, it could equally be argued that if existing resources were better spent (the Griffiths approach) then community care could be better provided. It is not a cheap option, as community care is not necessarily cheaper. The key to better provision is to be realistic as to what can be provided within the resources available. Priorities will still need to be set. We will still not be able to provide everything for everybody who requests it (and life will not be perfect after 1st April 1993!) but the community care system can be greatly improved within the resources we have available. Thus, better value for money will be achieved – which is where we started from.

> How do you feel about the recommendations that Griffiths came up with? In his place, would you have been saying the same sort of things? ... or something different?

Chapter Two

The White Paper: "Caring for People"

This document (which closely follows many of the recommendations of the Griffiths Report) is the key document for Community Care. The National Health Service and Community Care Act 1990 adds little to this document and is simply the legal means for implementing the White Paper.

Definition of Community Care

What would be your definition of community care? What would make sense to you? How does your definition match the White Paper's (below)?

"Community care means providing the services and support which people who are affected by problems of ageing, mental illness, mental handicap or physical or sensory disability need to be able to live as independently as possible in their own homes, or in 'homely' settings in the community. The Government is fully committed to a policy of community care which enables such people to achieve their full potential."

The White Paper highlights the significant growth in spending on social security to support residential care, from £10 million in 1979/80 to a projected £1,000 million ten years later. The reason why this is important is that it is probably from the changes in the whole system of funding of residential care – which has increased so dramatically – that the main finances will come for community care in the future. This is discussed later and explained more fully in Chapter 8

During the past decade, have you noticed this dramatically increasing spending on independent residential care? Has spending on other community care services matched this?

And what of the probable level of future demand. While the total number of older people will in fact decrease slightly over the next decade, the numbers of 'older' older people will increase. Since this group obviously makes more use of all forms of community care (health, personal social services, residential care, etc.), although overall numbers of elders might decrease, demand for services is most likely to increase.

There is also a strong probability of even greater demand because the numbers of older 'disabled' people is also likely to increase.

Key Objectives

The White Paper spells out Six Key Objectives for Service Delivery:

1. To promote the development of domiciliary, day and respite services to enable people to live in their own homes wherever feasible and sensible. Existing funding structures have worked against the development of services. In future, the Government will encourage the targeting of home-based services on those people whose need for them is greatest. This relates back to the changes in funding in residential care referred to previously. Therefore some understanding of how the system will work and the way in which it 'might' release finance for community care is necessary and will be discussed in Chapter 8.

2. To ensure that service providers make practical support for carers a high priority. Assessment of care needs should always take account of the needs of caring family, friends and neighbours. As long ago as 1983, the Barclay Report was pointing out that the vast majority of caring in this country was not provided by SSDs but by other informal caring networks. Barclay referred to the care provided by SSDs as 'a drop in a bucket' relative to that provided overall. It is therefore essential that 'caring for carers' becomes a high priority.

11

3. To make proper assessment of need and good case management the cornerstone of high quality care. Packages of care should then be designed in line with individual needs and preferences. More information on this in Chapter 4.

4. To promote the development of a flourishing independent sector alongside good quality public services. As recommended in the Griffiths Report, SSDs should be 'enabling' agencies. It will be their responsibility to make maximum possible use of private and voluntary providers, and so increase the available range of options and widen consumer choice. More information in Chapters 6, 7 and 8.

5. To clarify the responsibilities of agencies and so make it easier to hold them to account for their performance. The Government recognises that the past confusion has contributed to poor overall performance.

6. To secure better value for taxpayers' money by introducing a new funding structure for social care. The Government's aim is that social security provisions should not, as they have done, provide any incentive in favour of residential and nursing home care. This should herald the hoped-for move from residential care to community care.

General Aims of Community Care

These objectives are geared to achieve the following:

a) to enable people to live as normal a life as possible in their own homes or in a homely setting in the local community.

b) to provide the right amount of care and support to help people achieve maximum possible independence and, by acquiring or re-acquiring basic living skills, help them to achieve their full potential.

c) to give people a greater individual say in how they live their lives and the services they need to help them to do so.

d) to promote choice and independence.

The Key Changes Required

To achieve the six objectives, seven key changes are required:

1. Local authorities are to be responsible, in collaboration with medical, nursing and other interests, for assessing individual need, designing care arrangements and securing their delivery within available resources.

2. Local authorities will be expected to produce and publish clear plans for the development of community care services consistent with the plans of health authorities and other interested agencies. The Government will take new powers to ensure that plans are open for inspection and to call for reports from social service authorities.

3. Local authorities will be expected to make maximum use of the independent sector. The Government will ensure that they have acceptable plans for achieving this.

4. There will be a new funding structure for those seeking public support for residential and nursing home care from April 1993. After that date, local authorities will take responsibility for financial support of people in private and voluntary homes, over and above any general social security entitlements. The new arrangements will not, however, apply to people already resident in homes before April 1993.

5. Applicants with few or no resources of their own will be eligible for the same level of income support and housing benefit, irrespective of whether they are living in their own homes or in independent residential or nursing homes.

6. Local authorities will be required to establish inspection and registration units at 'arms length' from the management of their own services which will be responsible for checking on standards in both their own homes and in independent sector residential homes – see Chapter 7.

7. There will be a new specific grant to promote the development of social care for seriously mentally ill people.

NB: In addition, the Act also requires every local authority to establish a well-publicised complaints procedure.

> What are your initial reactions to these changes: do you generally welcome them, or only cautiously? Can you see any major implications for your job, and what are the training implications?

Conflict

It is obvious that in some cases 'conflict' must arise since, if people are to be given choice and the views of existing carers must be considered, then differences of opinion will exist, e.g.

1. the local authority assessment of need versus the views of the individual concerned

2. the views of individual versus the views of carers

3. the views of need as seen by different agencies (e.g. health, social services, GP, etc.)

> What possible conflicts can you anticipate that you may be called upon to handle – how might these be resolved?

Extract from Foreword to the White Paper

We believe that the proposals in the White Paper provide a coherent framework to meet present and future challenges. They will give people a much better opportunity to secure the services they need and will stimulate public agencies to tailor services to individual's needs. This offers the prospect of a better deal for people who need care and for those who provide care. Our aim is to promote choice as well as independence.

In conclusion, the implementation of the White Paper will lead to what Griffiths hoped for:

■ right services being provided at the right time to the people who need them most;

- people receiving help will have a greater say in what is done to help them and wider choice;

- people will be helped to stay in their own homes as long as possible so that residential, nursing home and hospital care is reserved for those whose needs cannot be met in any other way.

Chapter Three

Collaborative Working

"For the past 15 years policies designed to promote effective collaboration between health and local authorities have focused mainly on the mechanics of joint planning and on joint finance. Significant progress has been made but this approach no longer fits well with the Government's aims for the NHS as set out in 'Working for Patients', nor with its proposals for community care. The Government recognises that further efforts are needed to improve co-ordination between health and social services" ('Caring for People')

Thus did the Government set out its stall for achieving effective joint working, based on strengthened incentives and clearer responsibilities.

Reflect on a particularly complex case you can readily recall to memory. Who were the various agencies and professionals involved? Did they all need to be involved? Were there some agencies not involved who should have been? How would you rate the degree of 'collaboration' and how did it impact on the quality of care received by the individual?

Key Features of Community Care

Collaboration will be seen to be central in the following key features:

- Creation of a new and important distinction between the purchase and provision of health and social care.

- Creation of a single, accountable body or person with budgetary responsibility and control over the service provision.

- Creation of a devolutionary approach based on a shift of objective-setting and monitoring towards outcomes and away from process.

- Greater complimentary roles between health and social services authorities as purchasers of services with both aiming to achieve best value for public money.

- Creation of a more simplified statutory framework within which joint planning will take place.

- Establishing a clearer mutual understanding of each agency's responsibilities and powers, who does what, who decides what and of monetary flow.

- The creation of 'mixed' health and social services care packages and services.

- Creation of accountability systems matched to financial and contractual agreements between service providers and purchasers.

Local authorities are expected to work closely with relevant health authorities in planning community care services. As 'enablers', they may also wish to act jointly with district health authorities in commissioning care services. They will need to agree on common service specifications, conditions governing agreements or contracts with service providers and on how much each will pay towards the service(s) being purchased.

The basic principles of seeking to provide good quality care responsive to the preferences of service users and offering good value for money should be followed in any joint arrangements.

Roles and Responsibilities

As explained in Chapter 4, the social services authorities will invariably be responsible for the organisation of assessments and all that this responsibility entails. However, the health authorities carry equally important and specialist roles and responsibilities, such as:-

- Continued patient care of the population.

- Continued responsibility for health care needs of those who also require social care.

- Continued responsibility of regional and district health authorities for ensuring the provision of health care covering investigation, diagnosis, treatment, rehabilitation and continuing care, together with community health services, including community nursing.

- The role of the GP will also be a key role in the overall collaborative process through their 'first contact' position, their contacts with the wide range of related medical and non-medical colleagues and in knowing how and when to intervene through treatment, re-referral, prevention and health education.

- Clear, agreed local arrangements which enable GPs to make their full contribution to community care will be expected to be set up, thus avoiding complex and bureaucratic procedures.

- The Community Health Services and Community Nurse will also have an important bearing upon achieving the aim of ensuring that more people are looked after in their homes for longer periods. Community nursing services include staff such as health visitors, district nurses, community

17

psychiatric and mental handicap nurses who all have a wide network of help available in their areas.

- The role of the NHS in providing continuous health care will also be a crucial one in relation to collaborative working and community care and health service provision.

- Many people who enter long-term care within the NHS will require special care and consideration as will those people who may suffer from terminal illness and those suffering from mental illness.

All of these patient-focused services will require effective, co-ordinated and collaborative arrangements between several agencies and many individuals in providing assessment and service delivery.

Housing will also have a vital role to play in community care, in the area of more help and advice to owner-occupiers to enable them to go on living in their own homes for as long as possible. Adaptations and/or special accommodation may be other options with the same aim, working closely with housing associations, housing co-operatives, etc.

Collaboration or Confusion?

The impact and importance of such a range of options and the need for clear and collaborative arrangements cannot be over-emphasised and can be expressed diagrammatically as in the next page.

> What is your experience of collaborative working in your area? How would you describe it: effective, half-hearted, frustrating, a waste of time, or what? What obstacles can you foresee getting in the way of a really helpful collaborative working relationship in both assessment and the delivery of services?

National
Health
Services

Family/Carers
Social Network

Community
Health
Services

Housing Wardens
Sheltered Housing

GPs

Housing Agencies
(Stat & Vol)
Housing Officers

Community Nurses
District Nurses

Emp Dept
Resettlement
Officers
Emp Rehab Service

**Individual Client
'Case Manager'**

Community
Psychiatric
Mental Handicap
Nurses

Home Helps
Home Care
Assistants
Voluntary Worker

Social Workers
Field, Hospital
& Community.
Psychologists

?

Hospital Consultants
Geriatric Medicine
Psychiatry
Rehabilitation etc

Continence Advisors
Staff re Vision &
Hearing Impairment

Nurses
Physiotherapists
Occupational Therapists
Speech Therapists
Chiropodists

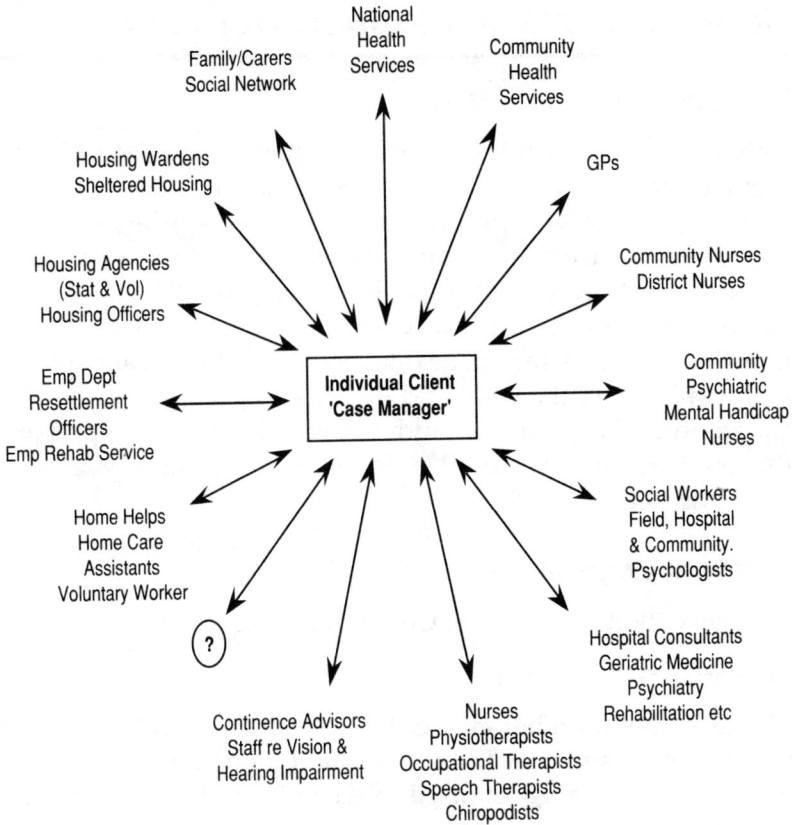

Consider all the players. Who is missing?

Chapter Four

Care Services & Planned Delivery

Introduction

Unlike the recent Children Act 1989 that superseded all the previous children's legislation, the National Health Service and Community Care Act 1990 leaves most other legislation intact. The previous legislation lays down what services a local authority and health authority should be providing, while the National Health Service and Community Care Act stipulates how these services should be delivered. The significant vehicle that would bring the what and the how together would be the Community Care Plan and authorities were obliged to prepare the first Community Care Plan for each local authority area by 1st April 1992.

Relevant Legislation

The legislation that defines Community Care includes:

a) National Assistance Act 1948

This was the 'foundation' Act for our present personal social services; it was part of Beveridge's ambitions for the 'Welfare State'. It is a very 'generalised' piece of legislation giving local authorities powers to provide a wide range of services for a wide range of clients but it spelt out very little in detail and hence left local authorities with wide discretion as to what they provided, for whom and on what criteria. It was a type of 'enabling legislation'.

The General Duty laid down by the 1948 Act is:

"A local authority may, with the approval of the Secretary of State, and to such extent as he may direct in relation to persons ordinarily resident in the area of the local authority, shall make arrangements for promoting the welfare of persons aged eighteen

or over who are blind, deaf or dumb or who suffer from mental disorder of any description and other persons aged eighteen or over who are substantially and permanently handicapped by illness, injury or congenital deformity or such other disabilities as may be prescribed by the Minister." Section 29(1)

This general duty has been made more specific over the years by the following legislation:

b) Chronically Sick and Disabled Persons Act 1970

This differed from the National Assistance Act 1948 in a number of very important ways:

1. It changed local authority powers into duties.

2. It made it a duty to identify need, provide services and inform and offer these to potential clients, rather than being a 'passive' service waiting for requests.

3. It spelt out many of the services to be provided rather than leaving the local authorities to decide.

NB: These all exist today although under different titles, i.e. practical assistance in the home = home care/help, etc.

However, despite expectations, this Act did not lead to common provision across all local authorities as they were still left with discretion in terms of

        (a) eligibility

        (b) amount of services

        (c) charges for services

        (d) basis of charges (if any)

Thus, although services improved considerably, there were still great differences among the local authorities.

c) Disabled Persons (Services, Consultation, Representation) Act 1986

The title explains the main provisions of this Act and it can be seen as an attempt to make the 1970 Act more effective. However, many of the provisions were never implemented as they have been superseded by the Community Care Act 1990.

d) Health Services and Public Health Act 1968

This Act attempted to provide for older people much of what was to be provided for chronically sick and disabled persons under the 1970 Act. Section 45 is very generalised, but a circular issued in 1971 spelt out in detail what the duties were. It is almost identical to the 1970 Chronically Sick and Disabled Persons Act.

NB: There is obviously a large overlap between elderly people and disabled persons etc.; many are eligible under both Acts.

d) Mental Health Act 1983

Section 117 (on aftercare) is a very weak piece of legislation and misses entirely the needs of most mentally disordered persons. Since approximately 90% of all patients entering mental hospital are 'informal' (voluntary) patients and since, of the remaining 10%, very few are admitted under the relevant Sections (i.e Section 3 (compulsory admission for treatment), Section 37 (Hospital Order by court) or Sections 47 and 48 (transfer from prison)), this means that local authorities do not at present have any specific 'duties' in respect of the vast majority of mentally ill people (including preventive work). Some local authorities do provide reasonable services as they have 'powers' under legislation to do so, but others are thin on their provision. The National Health Service and Community Care Act does attempt to rectify this deficiency by including mentally disordered adults in the Act and by making specific grants available for this group of people.

e) National Health Service Act 1977

This laid a duty on local authorities to provide home help facilities and a power to provide laundry facilities on the basis of illness, age and handicap. It also contained a power to provide day centres, meals, social work and residential accommodation to support people through illness and recuperation.

NB: A local authority may charge for any or all of the services provided under the legislation above. Charges must be reasonable and related to the person's ability to pay.

The Community Care Plan

Section 46 of the National Health Service and Community Care Act 1990 obliged local authorities to prepare and publish plans for the provision of community care services; the plan was to be a means of determining and communicating to the local populace how the authority intends to meet the social care needs of the population. In preparing their plans, local authorities were obliged to consult with:

a) district health authorities within their area

b) family health service authorities within their area

c) local housing authorities within their area

d) voluntary organisations within their area

e) voluntary housing agencies within their area

f) such other persons as Secretary of State may direct.

The first plan was submitted for 1 April 1992 and thereafter it has to be reviewed at least annually.

> Have you seen your authority's Community Care Plan? It would be worthwhile trying at least to find out what the Plan says about the particular service you are involved with. Also, most plans contain interesting demographic information which can be useful for a care provider in determining policies and priorities for the future.

Chapter Five

Assessment and Care Planning

It is not the Government's intention that anyone and everyone needing some form of care in the community should be referred to social services departments. People with exclusively health care needs which can be met in the community will continue to have direct access to, and receive service directly from, the community and primary health services. Some people's needs for social care will be relatively slight and they can be helped with straightforward advice and information. Some will have rights under current disablement legislation. Local authorities will need to form a view about when a formalised assessment process becomes necessary.

In terms of community care, assessment refers to those whose needs extend beyond health care to include social care and support, e.g. for mobility, personal care, domestic tasks, financial affairs, accommodation, leisure and employment, which they cannot arrange for themselves. For those people, social services authorities will be responsible for arranging an assessment of the individual's needs for community care, taking account of their problems, needs and circumstances. Assessments should apply both to people seeking domiciliary and day care services, and to people seeking admission to residential or nursing home care. *("Caring for People")*

Assessment – Government Expectations

"... local authorities, in accordance with directions by the Secretary of State, will assess the care needs of any person who appears to them to need community care and decide in the light of the assessment whether they should provide any services. The authority is required to take special action in the case of disabled persons and to draw apparent health and housing needs to the attention of the appropriate authorities.

An authority may provide urgently needed services without an assessment, but must carry out an assessment as soon as is practicable." (Section 47, National Health Service and Community Care Act 1990).

Central Themes

In relation to the assessment of client needs, the following considerations are central:

- the need to take on board the spirit of the legislation;
- emphasis on the need for accurate assessment ...
- leading to a service provision based on assessment outcome.

Assessment – The Local Authority's Aims

"The aim of assessment should be to arrive at a decision on whether services should be provided and in what form. Assessments will therefore have to be made against a background of stated objectives and priorities determined by the local authority.

Decisions on service provision will have to take account of what is available and affordable. Priority must be given to those whose needs are greatest. As part of its planning machinery, every local authority should monitor the outcomes of its assessment process and the implications of these outcomes for future development of services". ('Caring for People')

The key factors to be borne in mind when approaching assessment are as follows:

- assessments may not always be necessary
- assessment should be on the basis of what the individual can and cannot do ...
- ... and not whether they fit existing service
- therefore the service should be needs-led
- and should be available and affordable

- the local authority needs to define greatest need
- there is a need to re-appraise past assessment processes and current validity ...
- ... and to monitor outcomes

Objective and Principles of Assessment

The objective of assessment is to determine the best available way to help the individual. The assessment must take into account the individual's abilities, personal, family and social relationships and review the possibility of the individual remaining at home even if this means arranging a move to different accommodation within the local community and, if that possibility does not exist, consider whether residential or nursing home care would be appropriate.

The general principles that should apply include:

- Assessment should be multi-disciplinary, involving all the agencies and professions involved with the individual and his/her problems.

- Assessment should take account of the wishes of the individual and his/her carers and of the carer's ability to continue to provide care.

- Assessment should provide and support choices and self-determination.

- In some cases, assessment should allow an element of measurable risk.

- The assessment procedure should be flexible enough to assess a range of needs and issues.

- There should be individual and central case management and monitoring of the assessment process and outcome.

- Where appropriate, the individual and family/carers should participate in the final decision-making process.

The Organisation of Assessments

1. This duty will rest primarily with the local authority, but does not exclude other arrangements being entered into with other agencies.

2. Each assessment will/should have an individual case co-ordinator with skills in co-ordinating multi-agency contributions.

3. There should be a common process of referral regardless of the way in which the first contact/request for help with the authority is made.

4. There should be publication of:

   (i)   referral routes

   (ii) criteria for eligibility (for assessment)

   (iii) the process of assessment

5. The assessment process should be:

   (i)   as simple as possible,

   (ii) straightforward, not requiring elaborate and costly time-consuming case conference processes,

   (iii) cost-effective,

   (iv) as speedy as possible.

Before reading any further, make a list of those things you feel a comprehensive assessment should cover. How easy/difficult would it be to get this information?

---

6. A comprehensive assessment will cover:

Biographical details	Personal history
Self-perception of needs	Needs of carers
Self-care	Social network and support
Physical health	Care services
Mental health	Housing
Use of medicines	Finance
Abilities, attitudes and lifestyles	Risk
	Race and culture
Transport	

(Care Management and Assessment: Practitioners' Guide (HMSO, 1991), pages 55,58,59)

> Does it match your list? Can you identify the potential sources of the information you need.

Action following an Assessment

(i) The aim of assessment should be to arrive at a decision on whether services should be provided and in what form.

(ii) Assessments should be made against stated objectives and priorities determined by the local authority.

(iii) Decisions on service provision will have to take account of what is available and affordable.

(iv) Priority must be given to those whose needs are greatest.

(v) Monitoring of outcomes need to form part of future development and planning.

(Abridged:"Caring for People")

Care Planning – Individual and Community

1. Individual Care Packages. Once an individual assessment has been completed and a decision has been taken that publicly funded care can and should be arranged, it will be the responsibility of the social services authority to design care arrangements in line with individual needs, in consultation with the client and other care professionals, and within the available resources. *("Caring for People")*

2. This service provision should consider the appointment of a 'Case Manager', most usually employed by the social services authority, but not necessarily. The case manager should ensure on-going monitoring of the individual's needs which may reflect changes. Such a 'case management' approach is considered essential for targeting resources and planning services more effectively to meet specific needs of individuals.

> What would you suggest are the key features in effective case management?

3. Effective case management should include:
   - identification of people in need, including referral systems
   - assessment of care needs
   - planning and securing the delivery of care
   - monitoring the quality of care provided
   - reviewing client needs *("Caring for People")*

   These functions may be undertaken by different individuals.

4. There may also be advantages in linking case management with budgetary management.

5. There is a clear expectation that social services authorities will have to indicate in their community care plans how they propose to apply case management techniques and develop clear budgetary systems.

Case Study

Mr Roberts, a widower, is 72 years of age and suffers from a slight hearing impairment as well as a vision impairment in both eyes and, whilst not serious, does make communication and mobility difficult at times.

He is semi-continent and has just recently come out of hospital following hip replacement surgery. The GP, who can only visit infrequently, advised against early discharge.

Mr Roberts lives on the fourth floor of a multi-storey block of flats, where the lifts are often vandalised. He has savings of approximately £6,700 and receives a basic pension allowance. He smokes heavily.

Mr Roberts has only one daughter, aged 50 years, who lives nearby but who suffers from angina and can only visit her father when the lifts are in operation. She is on the telephone but he is not as he cannot hear properly and finds it frustrating, a waste of time and expensive.

Mr Robert's daughter has referred her father to the social services department as she is becoming increasingly concerned for his overall situation.

* * * * *

1. What do you think are the key needs in this case?

2. Which agencies/individuals could be involved and could provide a service?

3. How would you organise this process?

4. How readily could it be organised within your authority/agency?

Chapter Six

Managing Community Care

The local authority must move from its current dominant role of provider of services and become more a purchaser of services, dealing with as wide a range as possible of providers. The local authority's new role will become that of the 'enabling authority'. It will contract as a purchasing agency within what is now known as the mixed economy of care. This means that the service that the local authority wants to purchase must be carefully specified and then contracted with an appropriate provider.

The Purchaser/Provider Split

This concept first achieved some prominence in the Barclay Report 1983, and since then it has influenced what some have described as an 'internal economy' within the health service. In respect of community care, clear distinction will be made within the local authority between its purchasing function and its providing function. The local authority as purchaser will manage the assessment of the individual's needs, the care planning necessary for these needs to be met, the specification of the service required and the purchasing of the services that meet the specifications from one or a number of purchasers. The local authority may still function as a provider that is offering direct service provision through its residential homes, day and domiciliary day services. However, as a provider of some services, it will be in direct competition with private, voluntary and not-for-profit agencies.

As far as possible, the separation between the purchasing and providing functions within the local authority must be distinct. This will allow effective monitoring of the purchasing function and of the providing function, it clarifies staff roles, and it avoids conflict of interests. Obviously there are some parts of the social services departments which will find itself either not fitting anywhere comfortably, for example administration and training, or else straddling both purchasing and providing functions, e.g. a specialist residential centre that also provides assessment.

The Enabling Role

Once the assessment of need has been completed and a care plan designed, it will be the responsibility of the social services department to ensure that the agreed services are in place, and of the health authority and housing department (among others) to arrange the delivery of what they have agreed within the package. The local authorities must make best use of independent providers insofar as this represents a cost-effective care choice. Of course, as stated above, the local authority can continue to provide, but it is expected to take all reasonable steps to secure a diversity of provision. Thus the local authority "enables" care to be provided rather than being the main provider of care.

The role of the enabling authority is:

1. to identify the needs for care;
2. to plan how best to meet these needs;
3. to set overall strategies, priorities and targets;
4. to commission and purchase care as well as provide it;
5. to ensure quality and value for money.

A Mixed Economy of Care

Promoting choice and independence underlies all the Government's proposals for community care. It is axiomatic in the community care philosophy that people should be given a greater individual say in how they live their lives and about the services they need to help them to do so. But how in practice do you increase choice? The way the Government has chosen is in line with Griffith's idea of 'the mixed economy of care', i.e. seeking out and purchasing services from a range of providers in the voluntary and private sectors as well as the public sector. A key objective of community care is to promote the development of a flourishing independent sector alongside good quality public services and it is the responsibility of the social services department to make maximum possible use of private and voluntary providers and so increase the available range of options and widen consumer choice.

It is the Government's intention, through its community care policies, firstly to increase the proportion of independent provision of care services at the expense of local authority provision, and secondly to aim for a lower level of residential care support overall which will happen as a result of an increase in community-based support resources. How will this be achieved? There are clearly a number of strategies or forces at work, for example:

a) A powerful influencing mechanism will be budgetary control; care managers, i.e. those who will commission care services for and on behalf of individuals, will have capped budgets to work to – therefore they will more often have to consider the community-based resource option rather than residential care because the former will invariably cost less.

b) Residential care provided by the local authority will be more expensive than private or voluntary care; this is because clients in local authority homes who are otherwise eligible for income support cannot claim the residential care supplement as they would be able to do if they were resident in an independent home: therefore the local authority will have to make that contribution, adding to the overall cost.

c) Already there are currently estimated to be over 500 private agencies throughout the UK offering personal domiciliary care and cleaning services, and it is widely expected that the private residential sector will also diversify into this, perhaps offering 'mix 'n match' packages including domiciliary care, day care, meals, respite or holiday care, etc.; it is conceivable that some care managers may find themselves sometimes spoilt for choice, with the residential option possibly having less prominence than before.

d) The Department of Health's guidance makes the following order of preference in constructing care packages.

1. Support for the user in his or her own home, including day and domiciliary care, respite care, the provision of disability equipment and adaptations to accommodation as necessary.

2. A move to more suitable accommodation which might be sheltered or very sheltered housing, together with the provision of social services support.

3. A move to another private household, i.e. to live with relatives or friends or as part of an adult fostering scheme.

4. Residential care.

5. Nursing home care.

6. Long stay care in hospital.

In summary, the Government believes that client choice comes from offering the widest range of options; it also believes that maximum options come from a mixed economy of care; and it further believes that a mixed economy of care requires a flourishing and developing independent sector.

The White Paper, 'Caring for People', expects local authorities to take all reasonable steps to secure a diversity of care provision. However, the effectiveness of a mixed economy of care depends not just on the number of existing providers, but also on the ease with which new suppliers can enter the market, and local authorities are urged to encourage this. It is also suggested that the prospect of competition will have a beneficial effect on the behaviour of existing providers by stimulating them to become more efficient and effective. In particular, it will be essential for local authorities to develop the capacity to purchase places in independently run homes. No local authority should deprive those people assessed as needing residential care of the opportunity to enter an independently run home that meets the required standards of care. The corollary is, as stated in the White Paper, that all local authorities will need to review the extent to which they need to maintain homes of their own in these circumstances. Some rationalisation is likely to be required, although it is widely believed that local authorities will continue to be the main provider of residential care for the most vulnerable and most damaged in our society.

Service Specification

One way of promoting a mixed economy of care is by determining the clear specifications of service requirements and arrangements for tenders and contracts. The Government believes that service specification is likely to be one of the most effective ways of stimulating the independent sector. However, the Government is against compulsory competitive tendering in social care services – for the time being.

It is suggested that service specification will have a beneficial effect on local authorities:

1. It requires them to define desired outcomes, i.e. what is desired for the client, e.g. maintenance of independence, increased mobility, speech development, etc.

2. It requires them to be more specific about the nature of the services they wish to have provided in order for these outcomes to be achieved.

3. It requires them to define the necessary inputs, i.e. what is necessary to ensure the service is able to be delivered, e.g. premises, staffing, levels of qualifications, specialist facilities, medium to long-term business stability, etc.

Local authorities will be in a very strong position to use their new-found purchasing power to ensure high quality care for those who need it. Therefore, the quality to be delivered must be clearly specified as well, together with the ways of monitoring that quality. The specifications might usefully require service providers to set up and operate systems for evaluating their own performance. Again and again in community care, the concept of quality and the assurance of quality are predominant.

It is stressed that contracts and service specifications are not and should not simply be a means of purchasing the *cheapest* care available. There must be a means of identifying and ensuring that the best quality care is obtained. It will be wrong to make the specifications too rigid and allowance should be made for review and adjustment as priorities develop and change. All service specifications should also include information about the complaints and grievance procedures of service providers and social service departments and how to use them. (See Chapter 7)

In drawing up the service specifications, care managers will be required to identify clearly those aspects of the service which really matter for the customer and to specify those aspects as precisely as possible. The specifications will define both quantity and quality, for example, it may specify:

quantity	quality
staff numbers	staff qualifications and training
bedroom space	single/double beds proportion
number of places provided	key worker system
number of complaints	equal opportunities policy
number of day rooms	smoking policy
visiting arrangements	privacy/dignity afforded
staff rotas/routines	comfort and security
etc.	etc.

Have a go at drawing up a service specification for a client with whom you have been working recently. The following headings might help:

1. *Provider specification:* sometimes known as 'input' – what the provider has to supply, i.e. staff, buildings, equipment, food.

2. *Purchaser specification:* i.e. what the purchaser wants and how the purchaser wishes it to be delivered, e.g. special diet, physiotherapy, special care requirements.

3. *Client benefit:* i.e. the ultimate benefit of the service as experienced by the user, e.g. becoming more ambulant, speech improvement.

4. *Monitoring Quality:* i.e. how the purchaser will monitor the achievement of standards over time, e.g. monthly visits, quarterly review meetings.

Chapter Seven

Contracting and Quality Assurance

Why Contracting?

This is a political question and has been, and will no doubt continue to be the subject of debate. It has clearly been a thrust of the Central Government policy for over ten years and has gradually been affecting health authorities and local government in a variety of ways over that time. The claimed advantages of contracting are:

- it secures better value for money;
- it clarifies responsibility, thus making it easier to hold those responsible to account for their performance;

- it promotes quality public provision of service;
- it guarantees service user involvement;
- it leads to improved management and better utilisation of resources;
- it develops an effective partnership between purchaser and provider.

The concept of contracting is central to community care in that it promotes value for money, quality of service and customer choice. Virginia Bottomley, as Minister for Health, has said

"the aim of our policy is to make community care provisions more flexible and appropriate to people's needs, not to create unnecessary bureaucracy. All those involved in the contracting process must realise that contracts are a means to an end rather than an end in themselves. The purpose of the contracting process is to give local authorities the flexibility to develop appropriate and high quality individual care packages. Local authorities must, of course, ensure that they obtain value for taxpayers' money, but there is no reason for them to 'squeeze' the private and voluntary sectors."

Selecting Service Providers

Local authorities face a range of options for selecting providers:

- open tendering
- select list tendering (preferred suppliers)
- direct negotiation with one or more independent suppliers
- setting up a new organisation – as in case of, for example, management or worker 'buyouts'.

The main potential disadvantage of all methods of selection is that the selection of a single provider reduces choice to the individual service user.

The Contracting Process

It is obvious that service specifications accurately drawn up are essential in contracting. The process of contracting involves inviting the applications, vetting applications, and checking the credentials of applicants, for example their professional and financial standing.

Contracts are agreements which are enforceable in law by or against the parties concerned. In drawing up contracts, social service departments should take into account the provisions contained in Section 17 of the Local Government Act 1988 which relate to non-commercial considerations in contracts. If they intend to enter into contracts with companies in which the local authority has an interest, they should consider the effect of provisions contained in Part 5 of the Local Government Housing Act 1989 when these are brought into force. Contracts represent one means of safeguarding standards of service and as such should complement good management practice and underpin the work of the inspection unit. Authorities are advised to obtain legal advice when entering into any type of contract.

Contracts can be of variable duration, for example fixed term or renewable on a rolling basis. The contracts entered into should reflect the change in the pattern of service provision which the authority is intending to create. Time-limited or renewable contracts will allow the necessary scope for a flexible and evolving process. However, the need to maintain stability of service provision to users should also be considered in determining duration.

Contracts should be for the delivery of an agreed level of service for a specified price, usually for a defined period. Wherever there is a rolling contract, there should be provision for a periodic review (at intervals no shorter than a year) on price and other matters. The point of rolling contracts is to give stability of service planning to the provider as well as stability of care to the client.

Monitoring Quality

Local authorities are responsible for ensuring adequate systems are in place for securing the necessary quality of services and monitoring it over time. There are three main ways by which quality can be monitored and assured.

1. Purchasing

As was described above, services to be delivered must be specified in detail as part of the contract, and included in the contract is a provision for monitoring the quality, and break clauses if delivery is not as specified.

2. Complaints Procedure

Section 50 of the National Health Service and Community Care Act 1990 inserted a new section (Section 7b) into the Local Authority Social Services Act 1970. This authorises the Secretary of State to require local authorities to establish a procedure for considering any representations (including any complaints) which are made to them by a qualifying individual or anyone acting on their behalf, in relation to the discharge of or any failure to discharge any of the social services functions in respect of that individual. Complaints must be made by and must be in respect of a qualifying individual or be made by someone acting on behalf of that individual.

A person is a qualifying individual if:

- a local authority has a power or a duty to provide, or to secure the provision of, a social service for him; and
- his need or possible need for such a service has (by whatever means) come to the attention of the authority.

The consequence of this legal basis of complaints or representations is that any of a general nature, unrelated to an individual case, are likely to fall outside the statutory definition. Similarly, anonymous complaints are likely to fall outside the legal framework. However, it is open to authorities to deal with complaints not covered by Section 7b at their discretion.

The objectives of the social services department complaints procedures are:

a. to provide an effective means of allowing service users or their representatives to complain about the quality or nature of social services;

b. to ensure that complaints are acted on;

c. to aim to resolve complaints quickly and as close to the point of service delivery as is acceptable and appropriate;

d. to give those denied a service an accepted means of challenging the decision made;

e. to provide and define circumstances for the independent review of a complaint;

f. to give managers and councillors an additional means of monitoring performance and the extent to which service objectives are being met.

The complaints procedure had to be in place by 1 April 1991. It should be uncomplicated, accessible to those who might wish to use it, and understood by all members of staff. It should reflect the need for confidentiality at all stages.

There is a clear procedure that guides complainants through the process from the initial complaint to, if necessary, their appeal against a response that is unacceptable before a panel. This procedure is available to anyone who receives a service directly provided by the local authority or who receive a service in the independent sector contracted by the local authority.

No complaints procedure should affect in any way the right of an individual or organisation to approach a local councillor for advice or assistance.

The Mental Health Act Commission has responsibility for overseeing the detention and treatment of compulsorily detained patients and a general responsibility for the care, treatment and aftercare of all mentally disordered people who, together with their carers, may complain to the Commission.

> How accessible is the complaints procedure to your clients? Can you recognise any gaps?

3. Inspection Units

Administered within social services departments, the independent inspection units were established on 1st April 1991 and charged with inspecting and reporting on both local authority and registerable independent residential care homes. The units must apply the same quality assurance criteria to all homes. Inspection units will be concerned in the first place to:

- evaluate the quality of care provided and the quality of life experienced in private and voluntary residential care homes and in local authority establishments similarly providing board and personal care;

- ensure that a consistent approach is taken to inspection of public, private and voluntary provision;

- respond to the demands and opportunities for quality control created by the growth in contracted-out service provision;

- undertake their duties evenhandedly, efficiently and cost-effectively.

In addition to their inspection function, units may from the outset or at a later date:

- support and assist in the development of quality assurance programmes;

- provide a source of advice on the setting of standards for contracted out services;

- contribute to the quality control systems established to check that those standards are achieved;

- undertake the inspection of the authority's domiciliary and other non-residential services.

It will be necessary for arrangements to be made to ensure that, where the outcome of an inspection calls for remedial or other action, that action is taken. Clear rules concerning the preparation and monitoring of reports, including time limits, will be an important element. Follow-up action in individual cases may be complemented by – and may inform – a wider programme of advice and support.

Effective collaboration is called for between local authorities and health authorities in the management of their quality control systems. The district health authorities retain the responsibility for the registration and inspection of nursing homes, including those with which local authorities will, in due course, contract to provide care. They should therefore be informed of the terms under which a contract has been placed with a nursing home in their district. This will be especially important where that contract includes arrangements for quality control which may call for inspection. There will be common interest in these homes, as there is with those which are dually registered. Local arrangements will ensure that information about such homes, including inspection reports, is shared by the authorities concerned as a matter of course. The scope for joint working should be fully exploited. Health authority and local authority inspectorates will increasingly pursue common goals. This should be recognised in principle by agreeing and adopting locally a joint strategy, and in practice by developing shared working arrangements – including joint inspection and by combining training programmes.

Information which will be of interest to the inspection unit may derive from service users themselves and those representing them and from the authority's complaints procedure. Specific arrangements should be made to collect and use information of this kind.

> What aspects of a service give you some indication of the quality of care experienced by the client? For example, regularity of attendance at day centre, record of angry outbursts to staff, state of general health, calendar of social activities in residential home, number of complaints to home care organiser, etc.

Chapter Eight

Residential Care

The last decade has seen a vast increase in residential care provided by the independent sector, both residential care homes registered by SSDs and residential nursing homes registered by DHAs. There are currently almost 16,000 independent homes offering in excess of 350,000 beds. Parallel to this growth there has been a decrease in the number of care homes run by SSDs. There are now only around 2,250 of them left in the UK, and dwindling fast. It is believed by many that LA-managed residential homes will eventually care only for the most vulnerable and the most damaged in our society.

A New Perspective for Residential Care

The Wagner Report, "Residential Care: A Positive Choice", enunciated key principles for residential care which have underpinned much of community care's insistence on independence, choice, rights and quality.

1. People who move into residential establishments should do so by positive choice. A distinction should be made between the need for accommodation and the need for services. No one should be required to change their permanent accommodation in order to receive services which could be made available to them in their own homes.

2. Living in residential establishments should be a positive experience ensuring a better quality of life than the resident could enjoy in any other setting.

3. Local authorities should make efforts, as a matter of urgency, to meet the special needs of people from ethnic minority communities for residential and other services.

4. Every person who moves into a residential establishment retains their rights as a citizen. Measures need to be taken to ensure that individuals can exercise their rights. Safeguards should be applied when rights are curtailed.

5. People who move into residential care should continue to have access to the full range of community services.

6. Residents should have access to leisure, educational and other facilities offered by the local community and the right to invite and receive relatives and friends as they choose.

7. Residential staff are a major resource and should be valued as such. The importance of their contribution needs to be recognised and enhanced.

> What aspects of the current system of offering and providing residential care do you think compromise independence, choice, rights, quality care, etc.

The New Funding System

Although some residents are 'self-financing', an increasing number are not. It is this that has led to the dramatic increase in funding by social security that was highlighted in Chapter Two: in the 10 years to 1989 the spending on residential care by social security increased from £10m to £1,000m.

1. As from 1st April 1993 local authorities will be responsible for all admissions to residential care (except for hospital care and people able to pay themselves for residential care).

2. Admission decisions will be based on assessment by the social services department (in collaboration with other appropriate agencies)

3. If the assessment shows that residential care is appropriate for the individual client, then it will be the local authority (and not, as previously, the social security department) who will be responsible for funding the difference between the cost of the residential care and the normal 'benefits' available from social security department.

4. The benefits available to the individual client will be exactly the same in amount as those which the same person would have been eligible to receive had they remained living in the community.

5. Maximum use must be made of private and voluntary residential care sectors with local authorities acting within the purchaser/provider concept.

6. Existing residents at 1st April 1993 will have their rights preserved under the existing arrangements.

7. Respite care is included in these arrangements.

8. Each client will be assessed by the local authority on their ability to 'contribute' towards the cost of residential care. Various alternatives will exist as to the actual way in which payment is made.

9. In order for local authorities to be financially able to take on these responsibilities, the Government will transfer to local authorities (from social security) the resources which it would have provided for social security departments to finance care in residential and nursing homes.

10. The amounts involved during the next three years are:

     1993/94 –   £399 million (+ £140 million 'start-up')
     1994/95 – £1,050 million
     1995/96 – £1,568 million

11. In addition to being seen as more cost-effective and a more effective system in terms of residential care being used only following proper assessment, it is also intended to give 'choice'.

12. In order to ensure that choice is given, statutory Directions (Choice of Accommodation Directions 1992) are to be brought into force.

Choice of Accommodation Directions 1992
(amends National Assistance Act 1948)

- The first Direction is intended to ensure that people who are assessed as needing residential care are able to exercise a genuine choice over the place where they receive that care (to formalise 'good practice')

- If the individual concerned expresses a preference for particular accommodation or other accommodation (preferred accommodation) within the UK, the authority must arrange for care in that home provided:

  a) the accommodation is suitable in relation to the individual's assessed needs;

  b) to do so would not cost the authority more than it would usually expect to pay for someone with the individual's assessed needs;

  c) the accommodation is available;

  d) the person in charge of the accommodation is willing to provide accommodation subject to the authority's usual terms and conditions for such accommodation.

- The authority must also arrange for care in accommodation more expensive than it would normally fund provided there is a third party willing to pay the difference.

- If an authority assesses someone as needing residential care which is not otherwise available to them, it has a duty to provide (or arrange) provision of that care.

How do you respond to the following questions?

1. Will assessment by local authorities (rather than self-referral) lead to less residential care and more community care?

2. How effective will/can this be?

3. Will purchasing from voluntary/private sector on a contracting basis be less expensive whilst providing good standards of care?

4. Will the possible transfer of 'finance' from residential provision to community care be effective?

5. Will the 'Choice of Accommodation Directions 1992' provide sufficient safeguards?

6. What possible problems might arise from these?